Dedication

With thanks to Christopher for the
brilliant idea; and to Alyson, John and
Steve for their invaluable help.

Preface

Nothing exists outside of Karma.

It is a completely natural law, which pervades every aspect of every life of every person on the planet. It is compassionate, yet completely fair in the essence of love combined with the exactness of justice.

It is as gentle as the ripples on a lake and as relentless as the tides of an ocean. You can be at its mercy or use it to fashion your life.

Every thought, every action, every feeling you have is affected by your past Karma and affects your future Karma for better or for worse.

Ȣ This little book could change your life. All you have to do is open it at any page at any time and act upon what it means to you at that moment.

Ȣ

I know you can – I hope you will.

Introduction

✺

Destiny

There are many books about Karma and Reincarnation, but very few about Karma as a thing on its own. Most people think of Karma solely as something that was caused in past lives and that we are now creating the Karma of our future lives. This approach, which permeates much of Eastern philosophy, misses the main point: Karma is created every second of every minute twenty-four hours a day even while you are asleep. Yes, we are a result of our past lives – but we are also a result of what we did yesterday. Yes, we can build a Karmic pattern or destiny which will guarantee enlightenment in a future life, but we can also become more enlightened today.

✣ Astrologers, with notable exceptions, all too often reinforce the idea that we have an unalterable destiny. It is mapped out at the moment of birth in the alignment of planets in different constellations and there is nothing we can do about it. Of course good astrologers do not take this tack; they acknowledge that our destiny is there to be changed for the better in this life. Much can be learnt from astrology, but it is more of a guidebook than a bible. The daily stars in most newspapers and magazines, dividing the population into twelve groups based on just one of their signs (the sun sign), is almost farcical. Although to be fair, many of the astrologers who do these daily columns know this and skilfully use them to offer self-help advice with a little soupçon of divination thrown in.

⚘ Divination tells us what could happen, not what will happen. Divination of all kinds can and, I believe, should be used as a compass. It is particularly valuable if the practitioners have developed their intuitive powers, and can therefore provide the all-important element of correct interpretation. No matter how accurate a reading, the wrong interpretation can do far more harm than good. As someone who has given liter-ally hundreds of psychic consultations myself, I believe it is far more useful to give short and regular readings rather than one prospectus for life. A good intuitive can

⚘

then react to the changes brought about as a result of Karma.

 It is extraordinary that in the burgeoning industry of self-help manuals, so many of them are devoid of advice on Karma, which is absolutely vital, completely pivotal and utterly crucial - excuse the repetition but I really mean it - to all forms of personal development. I have written extensively on the importance of positive thinking, creative visualization, psychic powers, meditation and intuition, which are the building blocks of mental and spiritual realization, but ultimately even these will amount to nothing if the Karma is wrong. The good news is that there is an unlimited number of ways of getting it right.

Karma Yoga

જ⊱

I was fortunate enough (Karmically speaking) to learn from a master of several forms of yoga, Dr George King (1919-1997). Of all the branches of yoga he practised, including Raja (for mental and psychic control), Gnani (for wisdom) and Kundalini (for the mystic

જ⊱

powers), he rated Karma Yoga (service to others) as the highest and most important. This was, and still is for some, a controversial approach to yoga. Traditionally, Karma Yoga had been relegated to those who were not advanced enough to divorce themselves completely from material and family life and take the path of the monk or wandering mystic. The goal was to gain enlightenment by entering the profound meditative state known as *samadhi* as soon as possible. Some of them achieved this in a spectacular fashion, such as the eleventh century Tibetan yogi, Milarepa, who found enlightenment in just one life under the guidance of his master, Marpa. He manifested his mystical abilities by climbing the snowy slopes of the Himalayas wearing only a cotton robe, forcing him to draw on his inner powers or freeze to death.

❦ Dr King, who had himself entered samadhi after 10 years of intensive practice of the most difficult and advanced forms of yoga, came to a revolutionary conclusion. In samadhi, he said, you realize for the first time that you are part of an interrelated whole – this is no longer a philosophical theory, but it becomes an experienced reality. In that state, you are one with all life – you are no more concerned about your own enlightenment than you are about the enlightenment of the world as a whole. The concept of divorcing from others to find your own enlightenment to the exclusion of all else is therefore a contradiction in terms. Instead you should strive to change the consciousness and evolution of all life, finding your own enlightenment along the way. He declared this path of Karma Yoga, which is concerned with service to all, to be the greatest of all the yogas.

❧ In samadhi, Dr King frequently gained communion with other masters from this world and beyond. On one occasion in 1962 he received the following simple but profound message:

❧

You came not to be a slave of the basic Karmic wheel, but to be master of its every revolution. Evolution is borne from Karmic revolution.

This empowering approach to our individual Karmic destinies is very different from the fatalistic teachings you come across all too often. In some Eastern writings there is an almost defeatist attitude to service, as though there is not much we can do about the world so why bother. They point out that it is self-deluding to think you can radically change things anyway. I know what they mean, but I refuse to believe it. Look at Mother Teresa, Albert Schweitzer, Leonardo da Vinci, Mozart, Shakespeare, Plato ... you complete the list. And that's without mentioning Jesus Christ, the Lord Buddha and the other great spiritual teachers.

Success

If happiness is your only goal you will often be disappointed. Even if everything in your life was constantly rosy (an absurd proposition in itself), you would have to be a callous person indeed to be constantly happy while this world contains so much poverty, disease, starvation and injustice. The only thing that could possibly make a decent minded person happy would be to actively engage in doing something about the state of the world. And you do not have to be a genius to find something you can do to help improve the lot of humanity.

⚜ Since what goes around comes around, you will automatically help yourself when you help others. The division between self-ishness and unselfishness starts to break down and you enter a newfound oneness of purpose, which brings you success. Paradoxically enough, by foregoing your own happiness for others, you are likely to be far happier; and by merging your own success in a common goal, you will be much more successful.

⚜

Of course, there are examples of people who lead an entirely selfish life who seem to think they have it all. Let's hope they do not - otherwise they will have to learn the hard way in this life or a future one that they are responsible to others as well as themselves. To be successful, you need to manifest your destiny fully - and in some cases even go beyond it - by manipulating Karma as powerfully as possible. Along the way, you will gain knowledge, wisdom, a love for all life and, as a by-product of all this, happiness. You will also get something more lasting than happiness (which is a mental and emotional thing), namely joy (which is a heart and soul thing).

✤ It's no good me telling you what to do. If you want that, there are many religions that will do it. The Western religions, as much as the Eastern ones, are based on the Law of Karma. From Hinduism, which introduced the word Karma; to Christianity's *'whatsoever a man soweth that shall he also reap'* (Galatians Chapter 6, Verse 7); to Buddhism's *'for every action there is an equal and opposite reaction'*; to Judaism's *'life for life, eye for eye, tooth for tooth, hand* for hand, foot for foot, burning for burning, wound for wound, stripe for stripe' (Exodus Chapter 21, Verse 23) to Islam's concept of Judgement. The point is that every situation is different and has to be judged on its own merits. One thing you cannot do success-fully is to ignore Karma. It does exist and it does work in your life, whether you want it to or not, or even believe it or not. Just as your body operates according to its needs and limits, so does your Karmic pattern. The sensible thing to do is to co-operate with it, for your own advantage and the advantage of others. Trying to ignore it won't make it go away. Dr King once described Karma as pressure. It is there to be applied for better or for what may appear to be worse - and you cannot get a divorce from Karma!

✻ Denying Karma is foolish - accepting it is wise - obeying it is sensible - loving it is fortunate - and manipulating Karma is the key to success. This book is a series of one hundred little prompts for your everyday life. Although you may open it at a random page, it will not be by chance. If you wish you can make it more effective still by

✻

requesting guidance before you open it. At the end there are two meditations which, if done carefully and regularly, can change your life.

*⚘ Use this little book
    to create the Karma of success.*

The Meaning
of Karma

꙳

The literal meaning of Karma is *doing,*
which includes mental
as well as physical actions.
We are literally a product of our own
thoughts and actions –
that is our Karma.
We have made ourselves what we are.

꙳

Names for Karma

Moses called it God's Law.
The Platonists of ancient
Greece called it Destiny.
The Stoics of ancient
Rome called it Fate.
Mystics refer to God's Will.
Other philosophers have referred to it
as Necessity and Inevitability.
What's in a name? –
Especially when it is the secret of life.

Action and Reaction

To every action there is an equal
and opposite reaction.
You might not notice it for several lives,
but if you think about it, you will.

Sowing and Reaping

You've heard that as you sow,
so shall you reap.
But did you know that as you reap
so must you sow?

An Eye for an Eye

❧

You get back exactly what you put out
in order to learn what it feels like to be
on the receiving end.
It doesn't mean you should always give
as good as you get though.
Sometimes you can teach more
by not reciprocating –
by turning the other cheek.
Otherwise violence would never end.

❧

Sri Krishna

Perhaps the greatest of the ancient bibles is the
Bhagavad Gita. This was delivered by Sri
Krishna while driving a chariot carrying the
warrior Arjuna to battle. Arjuna no longer
wished to fight, but Sri Krishna told him to do
so - not as an act of war, but as an act of duty,
detaching from all results.

This is the spirit in which the Karma Yogi
should perform all acts: A willingness to do
one's allotted duty for no reward in this world,
with a dispassion known in Sanskrit as
vairagya.

Yin and Yang

The ancient Chinese recognized two
essential forces pervading Creation –
like the forces of Action and Reaction.
Yin is passive and receptive
Yang is active and creative.
Harmony is a balance of these two.

Does it Gel?

Sometimes things just don't gel.
You don't know why, but they don't.
At times like this,
listen to your inner voice –
you may be going against the Karmic
tide and it is trying to redirect you.

Buddha

The Lord Buddha said that right
thoughts and actions
could change Karmic curses into
blessings.

Calmer

You may find a little calm,
but with the right Karma,
you will be even calmer.

Accomplish your Goals

❦

You can achieve anything you
determine.
It starts with a thought and ends
with a result.
All the stuff in between
has to be dealt with,
so you might as well try to enjoy it.

❦

Casting the First Stone

Let he who is without sin examine
himself a lot more carefully –
there is definitely some
self-delusion there.
Let he who casts the first stone
be without sin,
but why not try something more
constructive than stoning?

Islam

❧

The word Islam literally
means resignation.
Surrendering to God's will is the
essence of Karmic good fortune.

Sri Ramakrishna

This saint who lived in the nineteenth century was known to give opposing advice to different disciples.
For instance, one disciple heard his master's name being mocked and was so annoyed that he got into a fight. Ramakrishna reprimanded him for his lack of patience.

＊

Another, who had witnessed this, later
also heard his master's name
denounced, but did nothing to retaliate.
Ramakrishna reprimanded him severely
for his lack of loyalty.
Each according to his needs.

＊

Dr George King

_❧_

Dr King described Karma as:

'The great Law; the all-pervasive,
irrevocable Law which is God.
Not that which is made by God,
but that which IS God.'

Crime and Punishment

Karma is there to teach, not punish.
The only reason we
are on Earth is to learn,
and Karma provides the lessons.
It would be criminal to ignore them.

Forgive and Forget?

Generally, there is far too little
forgiveness in this world,
but just occasionally, there is too much.
There are those who get the
wrong signals from forgiveness
and learn nothing.
Karma does not forgive or forget –
it teaches and helps.
It gives the right signals.

Jesus Christ

Jesus did not die to
forgive us our sins,
but to take Karma for
humanity. We should strive
to repay Him for this,
rather than asking for yet
more forgiveness.

Saint Peter

❧

Saint Peter was a great mystic who is
much misunderstood today.
He reluctantly obeyed his master's
instructions to the letter
by denying him three times when
the cock crowed.
At the right Karmic moment
he chose to die an even
more cruel death than his master.

❧

The Compassion Dividend

As well as being strict and unforgiving,
Karma is compassionate.
Despite all appearances to the
contrary at times,
there is always a way out of every
difficulty; there is always hope.
There is a dividend of compassion
built into the Law,
which you can draw on when you need
it most.

Abraham

As soon as Abraham was
prepared to sacrifice Isaac,
his son, the Lord told him
it was not necessary.
What you reject is laid
at your feet.

UFOs

When I was a student at university, I was short of cash and had to choose between buying gym shoes or books on UFOs – I chose the books.
Shortly afterwards there was a UFO sighted above the city by hundreds of people including myself. When the UFO left my view I looked down to the ground and saw a brand new pair of gym shoes there of my size.
What you reject is worn on your feet.

Heat in the Kitchen

Even though you don't like the heat,
sometimes you've got no alternative
but to stay in the kitchen.
When that happens,
regard it as a Karmic test -
that will at least make sense of the
whole situation and help it
to cool down.

Deds

Deeds

Do as you would be done by,
because you will.

Think Positive

Thoughts are things.
They have an effect on
the universal sea of mind energy,
no matter how secret you keep them.
Think positively and others will benefit
as well as yourself,
because they are part of universal
mind too.

Gandhi

A man approached Gandhi for advice.
In an act of religious hatred, he had
killed a person from another religion
and wanted to know what he should
do to make amends.
Gandhi gave him the following
Karmic advice:
Adopt an orphan of that other religion
and bring him up as your own.

Sir Winston
Churchill

Sir Winston knew from his youth
that his destiny would one day be to
lead the nation.
It was not so much an ambition as
something pre-ordained.
When he was driven to Buckingham
Palace to take his position
as Prime Minister,
he felt a familiar sense of what he had
always known would be inevitable.

Minimize your Problems

Look at the problems
in the world.
Is your problem really
as big as you think?

I don't think so.

Maximize your Potential

❧

You are perfect.
Your mistakes are lessons;
your disappointments are tests;
your failures are temporary.
You are perfect – so why not act
like it?

❧

Return to Sender

If you are on the receiving end of anger,
jealousy or resentment,
instead of returning it in kind, try to
send love to the person concerned.
The less you like them, the more
difficult it will be, but the more potent
the Karmic manipulation.
If they reject the love you send them,
their own energy will be returned to
them.

Prayer

One of the most effective of
all Karmic acts is prayer.
The next time you see a dire situation
reported on the television news,
instead of feeling down about it switch
the television off, raise your hands
and imagine streams of white light
going out from the palms of your hands
to the situation in question.

You do not have to be religious to do this - you need only believe in the power of positive thought. If you are religious, you can add another dimension to this practice by saying a prayer to your God.
You may help more than you realize.

Healing

Everyone can heal.
The palms of the hands are transmitters
of love energy - that's why healing is
often called 'the laying on of hands'.
You can heal people, animals and
plants by feeling love for them, and
transmitting healing energy to them
through the palms of your hands.
This will help others and be a powerful
Karmic manipulation for yourself.

Greek Tragedy

Greek tragic drama by Sophocles, Aeschylus and others was designed to show how powerless humans are when pitted against the force of destiny. There is no point in trying to fight the universal will – it only leads to tragedy.

Yogi Milarepa

✤

Milarepa had practised black magic as
a young man, which was common in
Tibet at that time. He later became a
student of the strict, spiritual master,
Marpa the Translator.
After some time, Marpa instructed him
to perform the same type of black
magic in a specific situation.
He obeyed, but loathed it so much he
never wanted to do it again.
The lesson was learnt.

✤

Environment

❧

Environment is not the ultimate factor
in determining our destiny.
Too many people have defied their
environment, upbringing and cultural
background and achieved greatness for
us to believe otherwise.

Finance

If you are going through an
unlucky patch financially,
change your luck
by giving something,
no matter how modest
the amount, to another.

Health

꒹

Healers often find that
when they concentrate
on the suffering of others,
their own ailments
also improve.

Relationships

Never try to possess another –
that's one way to guarantee that you
will lose them.
Set your loved ones free –
then they will be free to love you.

Give and Take

Whatever you give you will receive,
but whatever you take you can
never possess.
With a lot of giving and a little taking
you will get what you need.

Lessons

Lessons are life's way of making
you change.
Learning is your way of changing
your life.
They both work, but the second way is
quicker and much more satisfying.

Service to Others

You gain most
when you serve others.
It doesn't work when you do it
for gain though,
because then it's not service.

The Mills of God

The mills of God grind slowly but
exceeding small.
You can speed them up, but you can't
stop them.
So you might as well go with the flow.

Politics

No political system is the answer,
because the answer is not political.
Since politics is not based on Karmic
principles, it can only be partially
successful at best.

Pythagoras

Pythagoras taught his students to
question every night what they have
done wrong or left undone in the day.
This is a way of counteracting any bad
Karma by preparing the mind to
rectify it the following day.

Passion

✣

Pythagoreans were taught
to say and do nothing
while under the
influence of passion.

✣

Ideology

Political ideologies are all temporary,
because they are based on material
conditions, which constantly change.
The left wing in one country is the
right wing in another.
Generally they promote ideas of justice
and compassion which may or may not
be correct.
So does Karma, but it is always correct
– and it is permanent.

Responsibility

❦

We are all responsible for our
governments.
We are all responsible for the atom
bomb.
We are all responsible for poverty.
We are all responsible for disease.
Unless we are doing everything in our
power to change them.

❦

Omens

The beginning of an event
carries an auspicious
significance for its outcome.

Birthdays

Always commemorate your birthday,
especially by spending some time alone
in contemplation or prayer.
How you spend this day will affect your
year ahead.

New Moons

The new moon is the beginning of a
natural cycle.
Tune into this energy by spending some
time in quiet meditation.

Breathing

Breathing in is inspiration.
Breathing out is manifestation.
Breathing through the left nostril is
your inner life.
Breathing through the right nostril is
your outer life.
Like Karma, breathing can bring a
perfect balance.

What do you Want?

You may get what you want, but do you
want what you get?
It won't matter either way if you only
want what you need.

Medicine and Poison

One man's medicine is often another
man's medicine.
One man's poison is usually another
man's poison.
One man's medicine is sometimes
another man's poison.
One man's poison is occasionally
another man's medicine.
Best use your intuition when
administering medicine or poison.

Bread upon the Waters

Throw your bread upon the waters and,
if it comes back at all,
it will be so soggy as to be inedible.
Which goes to show that bread wasn't
designed to be thrown into water.
Apart from this, it's a great way of
illustrating that you only get back what
you put out in the first place.

The Matrix

꙰

All the elements of Karma could form
a multi-dimensional matrix comprising
thoughts, feelings, deeds, motives,
accidents, mistakes, successes
and achievements.
The computer to handle all this hasn't
yet been designed.

Judging and Being Judged

Being judgemental tends to make you
dissatisfied;
while a lack of discrimination tends to
make you moronic.
You never know enough to make a
complete judgement.
Karma, on the other hand, has all the
necessary facts at its disposal.
That is why Karmic judgements are the
only ones that are completely correct.

Signs of Destiny

Every culture has included some form of divination.
From the shaman to the native doctor,
the oracle and the seer,
someone has always interpreted the signs for us.
This is as true today as ever it was,
with a growing army of psychics and
diviners on tap to help in any situation.
It's only reasonable to assume
that there must be something in it.

Carl Jung

Jung, working in a stilted academic environment, brilliantly broke new ground with his concept of the collective unconscious.

He said: 'We may think we are following our noses and may never discover that we are, for the most part, supernumeraries on the stage of the world theatre. There are factors which, although we do not know them, nevertheless influence our lives, the more so if they are unconscious'.

Sounds like Karma to me.

Synchronicity

Jung formed his theory of synchronicity while working with the Nobel Prize winner Wolfgang Pauli, one of the twentieth century's greatest physicists, father of the neutrino and of the Pauli Principle that no two electrons can exist in an atom in the same state.

They defined synchronicity as 'the simultaneous occurrence of two meaningfully but not causally connected events'. They called it an 'unexpected parallelism between psychic and physical events'.
Considering that nothing happens by chance, it's not that surprising.

Wealth

There is no evidence that the ultra-rich are ultra-happy. Great wealth brings great responsibility and great potential to do great good.

Suffering

If it is someone's Karma to suffer,
should you help them or leave
them to their Karma?
Definitely help them –
your help will then be their
Karma.

Karmic Cycles

There are three major Karmic cycles:

aged 0 to approximately 30 –
for laying foundations;
30 to mid 50s – for producing the goods;
mid 50s to death – for reaping, not retiring.

How Karmically auspicious
each of these cycles are depends
on how you use them.
Each one can be a new beginning.

Minor Cycles

Within the major life cycles,
there are many minor cycles affecting
different aspects of life.
You may notice that periods of
good or bad luck are like buses –
they all come at once.

God Expects

They say that God expects more from
those closer to Him.
The more you have, the more you are
expected to give.
This is as true of knowledge as it is of
material things.

Guilt

It is not fashionable to feel guilty, but
without any conscience
there would be no limits to human
misbehaviour.
Of course, those who are perfect won't
ever need to feel guilt,
but they could do with a course in
humility.

Samuel Hahnemann

In the eighteenth century Samuel Hahnemann discovered homoeopathy. This system of medicine cures by administering minute quantities of medicines, which in large doses cause the very thing you are suffering from. In a similar way, Karma sometimes introduces painful experiences in minute doses to learn very big lessons.

Inequality

*

It is one thing Karmically
to harm a villain
and another to harm a saint.
Neither is to be recommended,
but there is a big difference
in Karmic terms.

*

Group Karma

As well as individual Karma, there are
various forms of group Karma.
The Old Testament speaks of the sins of
the forefathers being visited upon
future generations.
Some native tribes believe in the need
to pacify the elements due to the
conduct of their ancestors.

꙳

From families to tribes to nations
and the world as a whole,
Karma operates at every level.
Any kind of community or organization
is constantly creating Karma for itself
in one direction or another.

꙳

Love

Give love to receive love.

Sacrifice

Sacrifice in a good cause is very
favourable Karmically.
Whatever you give up, providing it is
necessary,
will come back to you all the more.

Remorse

Remorse is a useful way of knocking
sense into you.
Then it should be dispensed with and
replaced by useful, compensating
actions.

Regret

✿

Instead of regretting the past,
create the future.

Never Harm Others

'You should never want to harm others.
But, if you ever find that you do,
remember that you will also injure
yourself.'

W. C. Fields

On his deathbed, the long-term atheist
film star, W. C. Fields, started to read
the Bible. When asked why, he said he
was just 'looking for loopholes'!
There are no loopholes in the Law.

Animals

We are meant to look after and
care for the Animal Kingdom.
That is our Karmic responsibility.

Persecution

In our previous lives
we have been both sexes,
of many races and in most religions.
In the light of this, persecution on any
of these grounds is not only wrong -
it is base hypocrisy.

Transmuting Negativity

If you have a pattern of negative
thinking, introduce a new positive
thought to transmute it.
If you expect failure, visualize success;
if you expect illness, visualize health;
and so on.

Submission

There is a time to submit to destiny and a time to change it. It depends what life is trying to teach you at the time.

Failure

Make failure the start of your next
success.
You can only do this by recognizing it,
changing your outlook
and then acting in such a way as to
create the Karma of success.

Forgiveness

Instead of asking God for
forgiveness, ask for a way of
making amends.

Possession

You cannot possess anything in the
physical world.
You will even lose your own physical
body in the end.

Attachment

Mental attachment creates Karmic
attachment.
Mental detachment enables you to
lose it.
Spiritual attachment empowers you to
transmute it.

Schopenhauer

The philosopher, Arthur Schopenhauer,
wrote that the real significance of
co-incidences exists only in relation to
the individual who experiences them.
For others, these co-incidences pass into
the background of life and go
unnoticed.
What seem to be co-incidences are
really life's way of sending you
a message.
Keep an eye open for them.

Perfection

The Laws of Karma work in perfect
symmetry and balance
throughout the whole of Creation to
bring about the exact results
which are required at any moment in
every place.

Beyond Mind

The only force in Creation which is
beyond mind is Karma,
because it determines consciousness
itself.

Fear

Never fear Karma.
It is there to help and teach.
It is benign.
It is the key to evolution, growth and
lasting success.

What's to fear?

Bliss

When the Karmic moment comes,
bathe in the peaceful ocean of bliss.
It is always there for the taking, but it
will not fully satisfy you,
except in that moment when you
deserve it.

Charles Dickens

Charles Dickens' 'Christmas Carol' is a
Karmic tale.
When Scrooge became more charitable
and compassionate,
he also became happier.

Raja Yoga

This advanced form of yoga teaches you
that by rejecting all mind within you,
all universal mind becomes available
to you.

Debts

Karmic debts incur interest –
best repay them sooner
rather than later.

Preparation

'The day I swept not my house, the
master appeared.'
'Fortune favours the prepared mind.'

Two sayings which imply that nothing
should be taken for granted.
Always be prepared for the winds of
Karma.

Freewill

Karma does not interfere with our
freewill.
It gives us the freewill to give up
freewill.

Higher Beings

Masters, angels, avatars and gods
never force us to believe in them.
But every step we take towards them,
they take two towards us.

Thomas Edison

Edison tried many thousands of times
to invent the light bulb
before coming up with the real thing.
One of the Karmic tests is to see how
resilient we can be.
Sometimes everything seems to be
thrown against you to put you off
course.
If you have an inspired vision, follow it
to the end despite all the obstacles in
your way.

Service

The greater the act of service,
the more potent the Karmic manipulation.
The more potent the Karmic manipulation,
the greater the service you can perform.
And so it continues in a virtuous circle of
progress and evolution.

Posterity

If you achieve something beneficial to
posterity,
you will reap Karmic dividends in your
future lives
for so long as the effects of your
achievement last.

Speed of Evolution

We can either learn quickly or go
through lives of experience to learn the
same thing.
It is up to us - but why drag it out?

Pleading the Human Amendment

We have the right
to remain ignorant,
but it doesn't help our case.

John Lennon

John Lennon sang about
Instant Karma.
Wherever you go from here is up to
you.
Whatever you decide, it starts now.
You've got all the time in the world, so
don't waste it.
Instant Karma's going to help you.

Religion

⚜

Religion is not dogma;
it is Truth.

Mystical Powers

He who seeks mystical powers for their
own sake only gets them on loan.
He who seeks mystical powers to serve
others keeps them forever.

Encouragement

Give heart to those who are low;
you never know when
you might need it.

The Enlightenment Paradox

We are all heading
for enlightenment,
but only enlightened people
realize it.

New Age

There is a lot of debate about when
exactly the New Age will dawn.
We will only inherit this golden era
when we deserve to.

Three Karmic Times

Correct the past –
Discover the present –
Create the future.

Appendix

Two Meditations on Your Karma

Here are two meditations for those who wish to use them. They are specially devised to enable you to discover and enhance your destiny and have been tried and tested in my workshops. If you are not already familiar with meditation, it would be advisable to take a course or purchase a reliable publication on the subject before doing these exercises. Meditation is a way of going within to make contact with a higher part of your mind than the normal conscious mind, namely the superconscious. With practice, these exercises will have a benign influence on your life path and open the door to intuitive insights into your reason for being here and how to manifest it more successfully.

Preparatory Meditation

✣

Discovering your Destiny
Part 1

✣

Sit with the spine straight: if you know a yoga asana such as padma or the lotus, use it; if not, it is quite sufficient to sit on a hard-backed chair.

✣ Practise deep rhythmic breathing for a few moments.

❧ Try to make the in-breath and the out-breath as deep and even as possible.

❧ Make sure there is no tension in your body, particularly in the shoulders or neck.

❧ Allow the mind to become still – do not think about anything in particular, but just watch the thoughts float in and out of your mind.

Part 2

When you have done this for a few minutes and feel ready to move on to the next stage, put out a mental request as follows:

Throw light on my destiny; guide me on my life path; show me what is still to be done.

You can alter this wording to suit your own approach, but it should be along these lines. You are addressing your own higher self, which knows the answer to these questions.

Part 3

Allow the answer to come to you by watching the thoughts and feelings which come to you for a few moments. The answer may come in a form of words, in images or pictures; or just as a deep feeling within you. These are all some of the ways the intuitive mind operates.

You have to learn the difference between your imagination and your intuition and this takes time. So, if you are not sure whether it is a real answer or just your imagination (perhaps caused by fears or wishful thinking), do not worry. Keep an open mind. Continue with the practice regularly and you will find an inner certainty growing within you, which is your intuition. There is an entirely different feeling when you are imagining something and when you are getting an intuitive prompting, but only practice will enable you to be sure which is which. You may not receive any answer at all initially, but by putting out the request, the subconscious and superconscious aspects of mind will work on it and answers may come to you in a flash when you least expect them. Do not try to force or rationalize an answer, but allow the higher part of your mind to work it out naturally for you in its own good time.

Summary

This exercise can be practised every so often as a way of keeping in touch with the direction you are meant to be moving in.

If you try to move counter to your destiny you will be less fortunate Karmically than if you go with the natural flow of your life path.

The ancient Chinese sage, Lao-Tzu said:

> *'Returning to one's destiny*
> *is known as the constant.*
> *Knowledge of the constant*
> *is known as discernment.'*

Advanced Meditation

Enhancing your Destiny

When you have practised the Preparatory Meditation for some time, you can practise this more advanced exercise. It is important to follow all the guidelines carefully and not to lose heart if you do not get immediate results. One of the most important Karmic lessons life has to offer is perseverance. The purpose of this exercise is not to discover your destiny, but to enhance it in a particular way. You can only use this exercise for a worthwhile goal which you deserve i.e. it is within your Karmic pattern.

Specific Guidelines

⚜ You cannot use it to win money, at the races for example, because that would involve forces outside of yourself, and you should never use magical methods to attempt to control the actions of others. If you do, it will rebound upon you in a negative way at some stage. You can however use it to help you with your financial needs of yourself and your dependents.

 You cannot use it to make someone in particular love you, because that would be an attempt to interfere with their freewill, which is against the Karmic Law. You can however use this exercise to bring more love into your life from wherever it may come and, above all, give you greater opportunity to express love.

❧ If you wish to improve your health, you cannot use this exercise as a substitute for exercise or the right diet, but it may well help you to identify which health direction you should be going in.

❧ If your goal is not financial, emotional or physical, but rather spiritual – something you wish to attain for the betterment of others or to improve yourself – it will work particularly well.

Background

It is helpful to have some broad idea of your destiny from an astrological and/or numerological point of view. If you know your main star signs and where the key planets are or the main numbers governing your life path, major cycles and challenges, you will have some idea already of where your destiny is leading. You may have had some other form of divination or reading, but please bear in mind this will only be as good as the person who gave you the reading. Do not be ruled by it, but if you are confident of its accuracy refer to this also. Above all, draw on your findings from the Preparatory Meditation, which will have given you an intuitive idea of where your destiny should be leading. Do not practise this meditation until you have had some success with the Preparatory Meditation.

Part 1

❊

Breathe deeply and rhythmically with the spine straight, just as you did in the Preparatory Meditation.

Part 2

❊

Now, meditate on the following in this order:

stage 1: Identify what you perceive to be

your destiny - go through in your mind all the main points you are aware of.

stage 2: Distinguish between those aspects which are already manifest in your life and those which have yet to happen.

stage 3: Choose one of those aspects which has yet to happen and is a particular goal of yours.

You have now chosen the goal you wish to achieve and determined that it falls within the overall parameters of your destiny. Do not focus on particular circumstances in these exercises, but rather on a specific goal you wish to achieve in whatever way Karma determines.

Part 3

stage 1: Start to observe your mind. Watch the thoughts come in and out of your mind, but do not get involved in them, as though they were external to you and you are just the observer. This is known in Buddhism as watchfulness.

stage 2: Now focus on the goal you have identified, be it physical, emotional, mental or spiritual. Examine your life as it is now and then turn to the way you wish to enhance your destiny. Without bringing any other specific individual to mind, visualize the change you want to see in your life. Make sure that it is in all ways constructive and will not harm or interfere with the freewill of any other.

stage 3: Make the following invocation with gentle conviction:

I now request that my destiny becomes manifest with:
(verbalize what you visualized in Stage 2)

This invocation is made to your own higher self, which determines your destiny. For those with a religious faith, it may be made to a divine source.

stage 4: Now detach from what you have just invoked. Leave it in the hands of universal mind, knowing that what you reject is laid at your feet. Clinging on to someone or something is Karmically unfortunate.

Remember this old Chinese saying:

If you love something,
throw it to the wind.
If it is blown back,
it is yours forever.

May your Destiny bring you fulfilment.

Make your Karma bring you success.

For further information please contact:

Karma Service,
The Inner Potential Centre,
36 Kelvedon Road,
London SW6 5BW

Telephone: 020 7736 4187

Website: www.gokarma.com

E-mail: info@gokarma.com